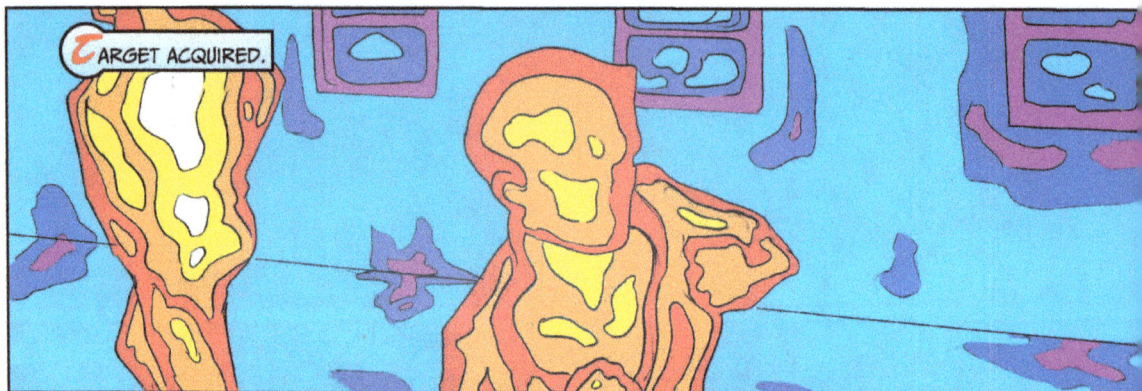

TARGET ACQUIRED.

SUBJECT IS ONE *ARNOLD ALOIS SCHWARZENEGGER*, AGED 7 YEARS.

THIS IS HIS DATE WITH DESTINY.

ARNOLD WILL NOT BEGIN HIS OWN FORAYS INTO THE GYM UNTIL AGE THIRTEEN OR FIFTEEN...ACCOUNTS VARY.

BUT IT IS HERE, IN THE LOCAL GYM IN THAL, AUSTRIA, THAT HE WILL TAKE HIS FIRST REAL STEPS ON THE ROAD TO MAKING HIS AMERICAN DREAMS COME TRUE.

ARNOLD'S FATHER, GUSTAV, WAS A NAZI STORMTROOPER, A MEMBER OF THE STURMABTEILUNG.

ARNOLD LOOKED INTO HIS FATHER'S WAR RECORD, FINDING NO EVIDENCE OF ATROCITIES ON GUSTAV'S PART.

GUSTAV MARRIED AURELIA JADRNY AND BECAME POLICE CHIEF OF THAL, AUSTRIA, WHERE ARNOLD AND HIS OLDER BROTHER MEINHARD WOULD BE BORN.

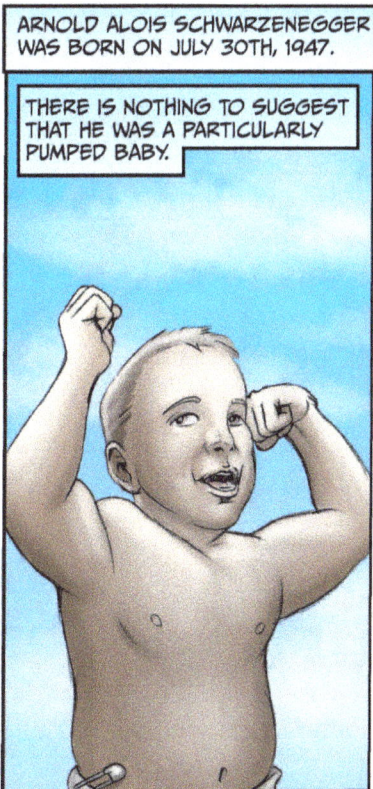

ARNOLD ALOIS SCHWARZENEGGER WAS BORN ON JULY 30TH, 1947.

THERE IS NOTHING TO SUGGEST THAT HE WAS A PARTICULARLY PUMPED BABY.

ARNOLD FELT UNLOVED BY HIS FATHER, WHO SEEMED TO FAVOR MEINHARD.

GUSTAV WRONGLY THOUGHT THAT ARNOLD MIGHT HAVE BEEN THE FRUIT OF ANOTHER MAN'S LOINS.

PERHAPS IN AN EFFORT TO WIN THE LOVE OF HIS FATHER, THE SOLDIER AND POLICEMAN...

...ARNOLD TURNED TO SPORTS. IN AUSTRIA, THIS INITIALLY MEANT SOCCER.

EVENTUALLY, HIS SOCCER COACH BROUGHT THE TEAM TO THE LOCAL GYMNASIUM...

...AND EVERYTHING CHANGED.

THE SEEDS OF ARNOLD'S PERSONALITY WERE SOWN EARLY...EARLIER EVEN THAN THIS.

WHILE NOT A MODEL STUDENT, ARNOLD WAS SINGLED OUT FOR PRAISE FOR HIS OUTGOING AND GREGARIOUS PERSONALITY.

EVEN AT A YOUNG AGE, HIS CHARISMA WAS UNDENIABLE.

...TO CRUSH YOUR ENEMIES, SEE THEM DRIVEN BEFORE YOU, AND TO HEAR THE LAMENTATIONS OF THE WOMEN.

THE SCHWARZENEGGER FAMILY WAS NOT WEALTHY.

THE SIMPLEST PURCHASES WERE CAUSE FOR REJOICING, AND ARNOLD ALWAYS LONGED FOR BETTER.

THE ROAD TO A BETTER LIFE WAS CLEAR TO HIM. ACTORS LIKE STEVE REEVES AND JOHNNY WEISSMULLER BLAZED A TRAIL FROM ATHLETIC COMPETITION TO SUPERSTARDOM.

HERCULES UNCHAINED

HE'S SO LITTLE!

WHETHER HE WAS DRIVEN BY HIS PERSONALITY, BY A DESIRE TO BE FREE FROM WANT, OR BY THE LARGER THAN LIFE EXPLOITS OF HIS ONSCREEN IDOLS... OR ALL OF THE ABOVE...

...ARNOLD BEGAN HIS PURSUIT OF A CAREER AS A BODYBUILDER.

HE WAS IN THE GYM ALMOST DAILY, LITERALLY RESORTING TO BREAKING IN DURING CLOSING HOURS.

HE BEGAN TO STUDY PSYCHOLOGY, HOPING TO TAP INTO THE LINK BETWEEN MIND AND BODY.

ARNOLD'S DEDICATION TO BODYBUILDING WAS ABSOLUTE.

UPON TURNING EIGHTEEN, EVER COGNIZANT OF HIS DUTY, HE SERVED A MANDATORY YEAR IN THE AUSTRIAN MILITARY.

DUTY OR NO, HOWEVER, NOTHING WOULD STAND BETWEEN HIM AND HIS BODYBUILDING CAREER.

DURING BASIC TRAINING, HE WENT AWOL TO PARTICIPATE IN A COMPETITION.

HE SERVED A WEEK IN THE ARMY'S JAIL.

EVEN THE ARMY RECOGNIZED HIS TRUE TALENTS, THOUGH, AND HE WAS REASSIGNED FROM TANK DETAIL TO...BODYBUILDING DUTY.

THERE WAS LITTLE TO STAND IN HIS WAY.

HIS MISTAKES DID NOT HOLD HIM BACK.

HE WON THE COMPETITION, MR. JUNIOR EUROPE, FOR WHICH HE WENT AWOL.

LATER, HE WAS RECOGNIZED AS THE BEST BUILT MAN IN EUROPE, A DISTINCTION THAT MADE HIM, IF NOT A HOUSEHOLD NAME, SOMEONE TO REMEMBER IN BODYBUILDING.

THIS LED HIM TO THE FIRST PLANE FLIGHT OF HIS LIFE... TO COMPETE IN THE 1966 MR. UNIVERSE COMPETITION.

HE PLACED SECOND. HE WAS NINETEEN.

ALTHOUGH HE WOULD MAINTAIN A GOOD RELATIONSHIP WITH HIS MOTHER, THIS WAS WHEN HE STOPPED BEING A FULL-TIME MEMBER OF HIS FAMILY.

HASTA LA VISTA, BABY!!!

HIS NEW LIFE BECKONED.

IN 1971, MEINHARD WOULD DIE, DRUNK AND DEPRESSED, IN A CAR ACCIDENT. GUSTAV WOULD DIE A YEAR AND A HALF LATER.

THERE IS ANECDOTAL EVIDENCE THAT ARNOLD ATTENDED NEITHER FUNERAL.

WHILE HIS FAMILY WOULD NEVER BE REPLACED, ARNOLD DID FIND MENTORS IN HIS NEW LIFE.

KURT MARNUL, A FORMER MR. AUSTRIA, HELPED INTRODUCE HIM TO GYMNASIUM CULTURE.

CHARLES BENNETT, A JUDGE AT THE 1966 MR. UNIVERSE COMPETITION, OFFERED TO COACH ARNOLD, GOING SO FAR AS TO PUT HIM UP IN HIS HOME AS HE TRAINED.

AS ONE OF THE JUDGES, BENNETT WAS QUALIFIED TO KNOW WHAT WAS HOLDING ARNOLD BACK FROM VICTORY: HIS LEGS.

ARNOLD IMMEDIATELY WENT TO WORK CORRECTING HIS TRAINING REGIMEN...

AND IT WORKED.

HE WON THE MR. U
THE FOLLOWING
TWENTY YEARS
EVER TO WIN

HE W
IT THR

IN
BO
PR
THE

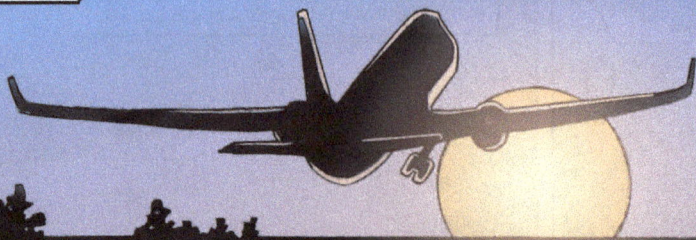

I'LL BE BACK.

IN 1970, HE DEFEATED SERGIO OLIVA, THE PREVIOUS YEAR'S WINNER.

I'LL BE BACK.

ARNOLD WENT ON TO AN UNPRECEDENTED STRING OF SUCCESS IN BODYBUILDING.

I'LL BE BACK.

HE WON THE MR. OLYMPIA CONTEST SIX YEARS IN A ROW, IN CITIES FROM NEW YORK TO PARIS TO PRETORIA, SOUTH AFRICA.

HE HAD WHAT WAS CONSIDERED AN UNBEATABLE COMBINATION OF SIZE, MUSCULATURE, AND DEFINITION.

I'LL BE BACK.

I'LL BE BACK.

AND THEN HE RETIRED.

UH...

BEFORE HIS RETIREMENT, HE WAS APPROACHED BY GEORGE BUTLER AND CHARLES GAINES, A PAIR OF AUTHORS WHO PENNED A BOOK ABOUT THE WORLD OF BODYBUILDING, *PUMPING IRON*, PUBLISHED IN 1974.

THE MOVIE WAS A SPRINGBOARD FOR MORE THAN ARNOLD'S SUCCESS.

LOU SMASH!

THIS SPAWNED A FAMOUS FILM OF THE SAME NAME.

IT INTRODUCED THE WORLD TO *LOU FERRIGNO*, WHO WENT ON TO STARDOM PLAYING THE INCREDIBLE HULK ON TV, DESPITE NEVER WINNING A MR. OLYMPIA CONTEST.

ARNOLD HIMSELF IS PRACTICALLY THE VILLAIN OF THE FILM.

HE IS PORTRAYED AS THE ARROGANT CHAMPION, WILLING TO DO WHATEVER IT TOOK TO WIN.

THESE WERE ARNOLD'S FIRST REAL STEPS IN THE DANCE WITH CONTRVERSY HE WOULD BE ENGAGED IN FOR THE REST OF HIS LIFE...ALTHOUGH HE WOULD ALWAYS LEAD.

HE REFERS IN THE FILM TO IGNORING HIS FATHER'S FUNERAL TO TRAIN, HE ADMITS TO USING PSYCHOLOGICAL WARFARE AGAINST OPPONENTS THAT HE DEEMED BETTER THAN HIMSELF...

...AND HE IS SEEN SMOKING MARIJUANA IN THE FILM AFTER HIS VICTORY AND SUBSEQUENT RETIREMENT.

WHILE THE MOVIE DID SURPRISINGLY WELL FOR A DOCUMENTARY... IT WAS A DOCUMENTARY.

NONETHELESS, IT WAS A START. *PUMPING IRON* RELEASED IN 1976... AND ARNOLD WOULD FIND HIMSELF IN MOVIES NOT LONG THEREAFTER.

MATINEE

NOW PLAYING PUMPING IRON

THAT SAME YEAR, ARNOLD WOULD HAVE A ROLE IN *STAY HUNGRY*, STARRING FUTURE OSCAR WINNER JEFF BRIDGES...

BUT ARNOLD TOOK HOME THE AWARD IN *STAY HUNGRY*.

HE WON THE GOLDEN GLOBE FOR NEW MALE STAR OF THE YEAR.

(THIS DESPITE A LEGENDARY TURN IN *HERCULES IN NEW YORK* FROM 1970... UNDER THE ON-THE-NOSE PSEUDONYM OF *"ARNOLD STRONG"*.)

BUT THIS SORT OF CHARACTER DRIVEN FARE WAS NOT TO BE ARNOLD'S BREAD-AND-BUTTER.

NO MATTER WHAT HAD COME BEFORE, THE REAL BEGINNING OF ARNOLD'S ASCENT WAS HIS STARRING ROLE IN *CONAN THE BARBARIAN*.

THE FILM REMAINS SOMETHING OF A B-MOVIE CLASSIC, NOTED FOR FAIRLY GRATUITOUS SEX AND VIOLENCE, AN ORCHESTRAL SCORE OFT REUSED FOR FUTURE MOVIE RAILERS (LIKE *GLADIATOR*), AND FOR ARNOLD HIMSELF.

THIS FOR A MOVIE WHEREIN THE STAR DOESN'T UTTER A LINE FOR THE FILM'S FIRST TWENTY MINUTES, AND WHERE HE ONLY SAYS *FIVE WORDS* TO THE FEMALE LEAD.

A SEQUEL, *CONAN THE DESTROYER*, WOULD BE RELEASED TWO YEARS LATER.

WITH THE GORE TONED DOWN, THE NUDITY REMOVED ENTIRELY, AND A MORE HUMOROUS TONE, THIS MOVIE DID NOT PERFORM AS WELL.

THIS DESPITE THE STUNT CASTING OF WILT CHAMBERLAIN, GRACE JONES... AND ANDRE THE GIANT IN AN UNCREDITED ROLE AS THE MONSTER AT THE FILM'S END.

BUT BEFORE ARNOLD COULD MOVE ON TO THE ROLE THAT WOULD DEFINE HIS FILM CAREER...

HE HAD ONE MORE SURPRISE LEFT FOR HIS *BODYBUILDING* CAREER. TRAINING FOR THE FIRST CONAN FILM HAD LEFT HIM IN EXCELLENT SHAPE.

ARNOLD, EVER CRAFTY, HATCHED A PLAN...AND RETURNED TO THE GYM.

HE KEPT THIS TO HIMSELF, GUARDING AGAINST A POTENTIAL INJURY THAT COULD PROVE EMBARRASSING...AN INJURY THAT NEVER MATERIALIZED.

ARNOLD HAD BEEN HIRED TO PROVIDE COLOR COMMENTARY FOR THE 1980 MR. OLYMPIA CONTEST.

AT THE ELEVENTH HOUR, HE MADE AN ANNOUNCEMENT:

SINCE I'M HERE...WHY NOT COMPETE?

FOR THE SEVENTH AND FINAL TIME, ARNOLD WON THE MR. OLYMPIA COMPETITION, THIS TIME WITH ONLY SEVEN WEEKS OF PREPARATION.

SEVEN VICTORIES WAS A RECORD THAT WOULD LAST UNTIL LEE HANEY WON HIS EIGHTH MR. OLYMPIA IN 1991.

BUT THE WIN WAS THE CHERRY ON THE SUNDAE OF ARNOLD'S BODYBUILDING CAREER. HE WAS THE ONLY SUPERSTAR THE SPORT WOULD EVER HAVE.

IN 1984, ARNOLD APPEARED IN THE JAMES CAMERON FILM, *THE TERMINATOR*.

THE DIRECTOR ORIGINALLY WANTED ARNOLD TO PLAY KYLE REESE, THE FILM'S HERO, BUT BOTH MEN SOON REALIZED THAT ARNOLD WAS BEST SUITED TO PLAY THE MENACING TITULAR CYBORG.

WHILE ARNOLD WOULD STAR IN FILMS THAT WOULD MAKE MORE MONEY, HE WOULD NEVER HAVE ANOTHER ROLE AS ICONIC OR ENDURING.

THE SEMINAL LINE, "*I'LL BE BACK*", WOULD BE LINKED TO HIM FOR THE REST OF HIS DAYS.

ARNOLD BECAME THE BIGGEST ACTION MOVIE STAR OF THE LATE EIGHTIES AND THE EARLY NINETIES.

HE LEARNED TO TAP INTO HIS NATURAL CHARISMA AND WISE-CRACKING SENSE OF HUMOR TO CREATE A PERSONA THAT HE COULD DIP INTO OVER AND OVER AGAIN WITHOUT PEOPLE GROWING TIRED OF IT.

EVEN HIS BAD MOVIES WERE FUN. (EXCEPT FOR *BATMAN & ROBIN*.)

HE MADE A BRIEF FORAY INTO DIRECTING, TAKING THE CHAIR FOR A COUPLE OF FORGETTABLE TELEVISION PROJECTS.

HE APPARENTLY DECIDED THAT IT WASN'T HIS CUP OF TEA.

CUT!!!

THERE WERE SEVERAL DIRECTORS WITH WHOM ARNOLD HAD PARTICULAR SUCCESS.

DIRECTOR

ARNOLD WORKED TWICE WITH PROLIFIC ACTION DIRECTOR JOHN MCTIERNAN, IN *PREDATOR* AND THE *LAST ACTION HERO*.

AND HE DID THREE WELL-RECEIVED COMEDIES WITH *GHOSTBUSTERS* DIRECTOR IVAN REITMAN.

BUT HIS BEST AND MOST LUCRATIVE COLLABORATIONS WERE WITH ONE GUY IN PARTICULAR.

MY FRIEND JAMES CAMERON AND I MADE THREE FILMS TOGETHER - *TRUE LIES, THE TERMINATOR* AND *TERMINATOR 2*.

OF COURSE, THAT WAS DURING HIS EARLY, LOW- BUDGET, ART- HOUSE PERIOD.

BUT HE WAS WITHOUT JAMES CAMERON FOR HIS FINAL TIME DONNING THE TERMINATOR'S LEATHERS.

TERMINATOR 3: RISE OF THE MACHINES DID FAIRLY WELL IN THE BOX OFFICE, BUT WAS WIDELY PANNED AS THE WORST FILM OF THE SERIES TO THAT POINT.

AND WHILE IT WOULD NOT BE ARNOLD'S LAST APPEARANCE ONSCREEN, IT ESSENTIALLY MARKED THE END OF HIS CAREER AS A LEADING MAN.

BUT AS WITH EVERYTHING ELSE, THAT WAS BY DESIGN. HIS CAREER WAS ABOUT TO TAKE YET ANOTHER TURN.

ARNOLD'S RELATIONSHIP WITH AMERICAN POLITICS BEGAN RELATIVELY EARLY, WHILE WATCHING RICHARD NIXON RUNNING FOR PRESIDENT.

ARNOLD HAD BEEN IN AMERICA LESS THAN A YEAR, AND HE HAD COME BECAUSE IT WAS A LAND OF OPPORTUNITY, A LAND OF FREE ENTERPRISE AND LOW TAXES...AT LEAST COMPARED TO THE EUROPE HE HAD JUST LEFT.

WITH THAT, ARNOLD DECIDED HE WAS A REPUBLICAN.

HIS FILMS HAD A CERTAIN PRO-MILITARY BENT TO THEM, AND HE WAS SOON SEEN SHAKING HANDS WITH A LOT OF PROMINENT REPUBLICANS.

HE WAS IN AN ANTI-DRUG VIDEO PUT TOGETHER BY THE REAGAN ADMINISTRATION...

HIS POLITICAL LEANINGS WERE NO SECRET...BUT THE WATERS WERE MUDDIED WHEN HE MARRIED MARIA SHRIVER IN 1986.

A BROADCAST JOURNALIST FOR CBS AND NBC, SHE ALSO HAPPENED TO BE ONE OF THE KENNEDYS, NIECE TO THE LATE PRESIDENT.

SHE WAS OBVIOUSLY A REGISTERED DEMOCRAT.

ARNOLD HAS BEEN FREQUENTLY ACCUSED OF MISCONDUCT WITH WOMEN, AND THERE IS SOME... CROSSOVER...IN TERMS OF THE LONG-TERM RELATIONSHIPS LEADING UP TO HIS MARRIAGE.

BUT HIS MARRIAGE, LIKE HE HIMSELF, IS OF TEFLON. ARNOLD HAS NEVER PUT UP MUCH OF A FIGHT AGAINST ALLEGATIONS, NOR SEEMED LIKE HE FELT GUILTY ABOUT ANYTHING.

...AND HE SERVED AS CHAIRMAN OF THE PRESIDENT'S COUNCIL ON PHYSICAL FITNESS AND SPORTS UNDER THE FIRST PRESIDENT BUSH.

AND HIS MARRIAGE HAS NEVER SEEMED ANYTHING BUT HAPPY TO THE PUBLIC.

ON AUGUST 6, 2003, WITH *TERMINATOR 3* STILL IN THEATERS, ARNOLD WENT ON THE TONIGHT SHOW WITH JAY LENO...

....AND ANNOUNCED THAT HE WAS ENTERING THE RECALL ELECTION AS A CANDIDATE TO UNSEAT CALIFORNIA GOVERNOR GRAY DAVIS.

FITTINGLY, IT WASN'T LONG UNTIL THE MOVIE PUNS STARTED.

DUBBED "THE GOVERNATOR" AND "THE RUNNING MAN" (AFTER A FILM IN WHICH HE COINCIDENTALLY SHARED THE SCREEN WITH FUTURE MINNESOTA GOVERNOR JESSE VENTURA), HIS CAMPAIGN WAS A MEDIA SENSATION.

THE UNPOPULAR DAVIS' OUSTER WAS PRACTICALLY A FOREGONE CONCLUSION, AND ARNOLD WON THE ELECTION ON BY A 1.3 MILLION VOTE MARGIN.

ARNOLD WAS HARDLY THE ONLY CELEBRITY OR UNCONVENTIONAL CANDIDATE.

BILLBOARD *MAVEN ANGELYNE, GARY COLEMAN,* HUSTLER PUBLISHER *LARRY FLYNT,* PORN STAR *MARY CAREY,* AND COMEDIAN *LEO GALLAGHER,* TO NAME A FEW, ADDED THEMSELVES TO THE BALLOT.

ALL OF THE FREAKS ON THE BALLOT PROBABLY DID NOT APPRECIABLY HURT THE CANDIDACIES OF *CRUZ BUSTAMANTE* OR *TOM McCLINTOCK,* THE NEXT TWO TOP VOTE-GETTERS...

NOT TO MENTION HONEST-TO-GOD POLITICIANS...

BUT THEY DIDN'T HELP, EITHER.

ARNOLD MAY HAVE BEEN A CELEBRITY AND AN UNCONVENTIONAL CHOICE, BUT HIS INCREDIBLE WORK ETHIC AND DRIVE WERE IMMEDIATELY APPARENT...

...AS WERE HIS ABILITIES TO BOTH CHARM AND ALIENATE THE PUBLIC.

IN NOVEMBER 2005, THE GOVERNOR CALLED A SPECIAL ELECTION, PUSHING FORTH INITIATIVES THAT HE CHAMPIONED, INCLUDING SUCH THINGS AS STATE SPENDING LIMITS, AND REQUIREMENTS FOR MINORS TO INFORM PARENTS BEFORE HAVING ABORTIONS.

HIS REPEAL OF UNPOPULAR INCREASES IN FEES AT THE DMV AND HIS BAN ON THE LICENSING OF ILLEGAL IMMIGRANTS WERE PRETTY MUCH NO-BRAINERS, AND WENT OVER WELL.

LOBBYISTS SPENT HUNDREDS OF MILLIONS IN OPPOSITION, AND ALL EIGHT OF THE INITIATIVES ON THE BALLOT FAILED.

EVEN A BRIEF BUT WELL-PUBLICIZED FLAP OVER HIM CALLING DEMOCRATS IN THE STATE LEGISLATURE "GIRLIE-MEN", AFTER A POPULAR *SATURDAY NIGHT LIVE* SKETCH, SUCCEEDED IN MAKING HIS OPPONENTS LOOK LIKE EXACTLY THAT.

IT WAS ARGUABLY THE WORST DEFEAT OF ANY OF ARNOLD'S CAREERS.

NONETHELESS, ARNOLD RETAINED MUCH OF HIS POPULARITY.

HE KNEW PRECISELY WHEN TO SUPPORT AND WHEN TO BREAK FROM THE UNPOPULAR ADMINISTRATION OF THE SECOND PRESIDENT BUSH.

UNLIKE OTHER SELF-PROFESSED MAVERICKS AND NON-PARTISANS, ARNOLD HAS NEVER COMPLETELY TOED THE LINE OF THE REPUBLICAN PARTY.

HE HAS OFTEN COME OFF AS A SOCIAL LIBERAL, AND HAS WORKED HARD TO MAKE CALIFORNIA ONE OF THE LEADERS IN THE GREEN MOVEMENT.

THE TRUTH OF THE MATTER IS, ARNOLD SCWARZENEGGER HAS HAD A PLAN FROM THE BEGINNING, AND HAS EXECUTED IT BRILLIANTLY.

FROM A VERY YOUNG AGE, HE HAS KNOWN WHAT HE WANTED TO DO.

HERCULES UNCHAINED

IT WAS ALWAYS A PART OF THE PLAN FOR HIM TO PARLAY SUCCESS AS AN ATHLETE INTO SUCCESS AS A BUSINESSMAN AND A MOVIE STAR.

$

ARNOLD'S SUCCESSES IN THE BUSINESS WORLD ARE QUIET ONES, NOT THE SORT THAT MAKE HEADLINES.

(UNLESS YOU COUNT HIS TENURE AS A CO-OWNER OF PLANET HOLLYWOOD.)

BETWEEN REAL ESTATE AND HIS BUSINESSES, ARNOLD WAS A MILLIONAIRE EVEN BEFORE HIS FILM CAREER TOOK OFF.

ARNOLD IS A WEALTHY MAN, WEALTHY ENOUGH TO HAVE BOUGHT A PRIVATE PLANE OUT OF POCKET.

HIS FINANCIAL PHILOSOPHIES ARE SIMPLE.

MONEY DOESN'T MAKE YOU HAPPY. I NOW HAVE $50 MILLION, BUT I WAS JUST AS HAPPY WHEN I HAD $48 MILLION.

ONLY ONE ITEM ON HIS LIST LEFT TO CHECK OFF.

IT'S AN UPHILL BATTLE.

THE CONSTITUTION IS CLEAR:

We the People of the

Article I

"NO PERSON EXCEPT A NATURAL BORN CITIZEN, OR A CITIZEN OF THE UNITED STATES, AT THE TIME OF THE ADOPTION OF THIS CONSTITUTION, SHALL BE ELIGIBLE TO THE OFFICE OF PRESIDENT..."

HE WAS BORN IN THE WRONG PLACE, OR AT THE WRONG TIME...

...BUT THE BEAUTY OF THE CONSTITUTION IS THAT IT CAN BE CHANGED. AND TRADITIONALLY, IT HAS CHANGED TO MAKE US A FREER SOCIETY, BOUND LESS AND LESS TO THE CIRCUMSTANCES OF OUR BIRTH.

ARNOLD SURELY KNOWS THIS. HE'S COUNTING ON IT.

COULD THE SON OF AN AUSTRIAN MEMBER OF THE NAZI PARTY ONE DAY BE A SERIOUS CONTENDER FOR THE HIGHEST OFFICE IN THE UNITED STATES?

YOU CAN BE SURE THAT THIS IS A QUESTION THAT WILL BE ASKED ON A NATIONAL STAGE IN THE NOT-TOO-DISTANT FUTURE.

THERE IS NO QUESTION THAT THERE WILL BE OPPOSITION BOTH WITHIN AND WITHOUT HIS PARTY.

MOST REPUBLICANS AREN'T KEEN ON A CANDIDATE WHO TENDS TO BE PRO-CHOICE, GREEN, AND IS MARRIED TO A KENNEDY.

AND MOST DEMOCRATS AREN'T KEEN ON A REPUBLICAN, NO MATTER HOW MODERATE.

BUT ARNOLD HAS BEATEN LONG ODDS OVER AND OVER AGAIN.

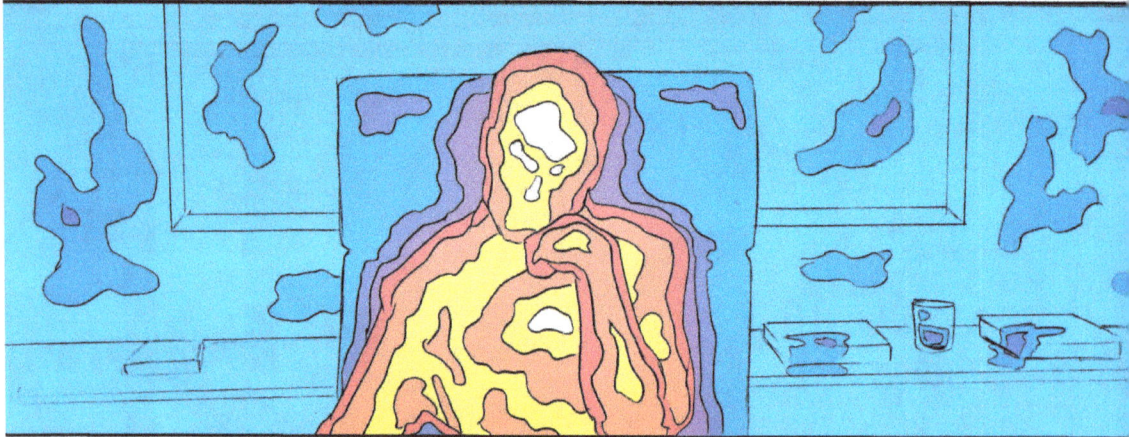

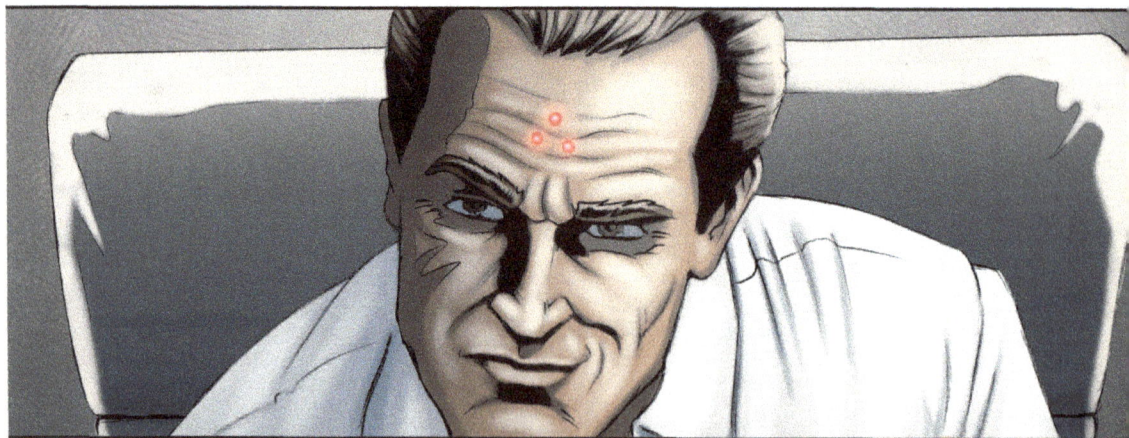

‹THIS SCHWARZENEGGER IS TOO DIFFICULT PREY.›

‹I WILL SEEK A DIFFERENT TARGET.›

‹PERHAPS DANNY GLOVER?›

THE END

BLUEWATER COMICS

JUNE '10
1

★ POLITICAL ★ POWER ★

Arnold Schwarzenegger

Justin Peniston — Writer

Matt Filer — Penciler

Kirsty Swan — Colorist

Wilson Ramos Jr. — Letterer

Darren G. Davis — Graphics

Cover: Deborah Max

Patrick Foster
Logo Design

Adam Ellis
Production

Darren G. Davis
Publisher

Jason Schultz
Vice President

Lisa K. Brause
Entertainment Manager

Crystal VanDiver
Director

Lisa Battan
Marketing Director

Janda Tithia
Coordinator

Scott Davis
Media Manager

Kim Sherman
Marketing Director

Vonnie Harris
New Business

Adam Ellis
Coordinator

BLUEWATER COMICS

www.bluewaterprod.com

www.ingramcontent.com/pod-product-compliance
Lightning Source LLC
Chambersburg PA
CBHW081236020426
42331CB00012B/3197